I0409902

TABLE OF CONTENTS

EXECUTIVE SUMMARY

Title: **PRIVATE MILITIAS: THE CANCER OF THE AMERICAN SOCIETY**

Author: Major Henry J. Domingue, Jr., United States Marine Corps

Thesis: Private militias and other extremist right-wing organizations operating within the United States pose a very real threat to American citizens and to other segments of society, because, taken collectively, militias are breeding grounds for radical followers--Right-wing extremists who are paranoid and prone to violence. However, since violent extremists only make up a small percentage of the militias, and the ability to sustain long-term cooperation or unity of effort is low, the militia movement will not be enough to threaten the larger national security of the United States.

Background: Militias and various other right-wing groups pose a disturbing threat to the American public. These right-wing organizations include the Ku Klux Klan, neo-Nazis, the Aryan Nations, but the groups that pose the most significant threat are the private, citizen militias operating within the United States today. These various organizations may share such common beliefs as racial purity, anti-Semitism, anti-abortion, opposition to taxation and pro individual rights. However, the two biggest beliefs are strong 2nd amendment rights and the intense hatred and distrust of the federal government.

Most militias, and the members therein, do not pose a threat of terrorist-style violence, but there is a small but active segment (the radical fringe) that seeks to convey their message through violence. It is their acute paranoia, coupled with access to illegal weapons and explosives that makes the radical fringe so dangerous to American society. Arson, assassination, chemical and biological contamination and explosive destruction of buildings and installations are their capabilities.

Within the extremist, right-wing subculture, individuals have migrated between other types of right-wing organizations. Recently, the trend has been for ultra extremists and white supremacists to affiliate themselves with the militia movement in order to share in the limited public legitimacy of militias in general. This newly established doctrine allows believers to fuse hate with conspiracy theories and the widespread distrust of the federal government, a truly volatile mixture.

Nevertheless, militias in the U. S. possess neither the adequate strength in numbers to be a viable threat to the nation, nor are they able to collectively stay focused with one common voice.

Conclusion: As long as the federal government continues in its present scope and capacity, militias and other right-wing organizations will continue to exist in opposition to the government. Furthermore, while the overall threat that private militias pose to national security is low, militia violence will remain a viable threat to American society for the foreseeable future.

I   INTRODUCTION

"The militia MUST pose a tremendous threat to tyrants and terrorists who hide within the government…One may ask, 'Who would have the power to throw off such Government?' The citizen militia of course…The citizen militia are the citizens protecting themselves."[1]

Norm Olsen, leader of the
Northern Michigan Regional Militia

Beginning in the 1990s and continuing into the 21st century, the increase in domestic terrorism has been linked to the rise in the anti-government sentiment, specifically caused by the rise of the private militia movement. While the majority of militias operating within the United States are non-violent, there are a small percentage of members, the <u>radical fringe</u>, who commit acts of violence to advance their ideological goals. The radical fringe frequently takes extreme measures against federal authority, taxation, race relations, and abortion, and they are fanatical believers of individual rights, and conservative interpretation of the bible.

Militia groups gained widespread attention from the Oklahoma City (OKC) bombing in 1995, and even though they were not members of a militia, it was the actions of Timothy McVeigh and Terry Nichols that focused the American public's attention on the potential threat of private militias. Currently, the FBI classifies militia groups within four categories, ranging from moderate groups that do not engage in

---

[1]Mack Mariani, "The Michigan Militia: Political Engagement or Political Alienation," *Terrorism and Political Violence* (London: Frank Cass Publisher), 10, no. 4, (Winter 1998), 125.

criminal activity to radical cells, which commit violent acts of terrorism.[2] But to properly assess the potential for radical, militia violence, it is important to size up the threat quantifiably and qualitatively. In 2001, militias and other extremist, right-wing organizations do not possess the sufficient strength to be considered a threat to the integrity of this nation. However, there are enough individuals--either members of an established militia or members of the radical fringe--who distrust and hate the federal government and its officials enough to commit violent acts of domestic terrorism.

As stated by Norm Olsen, "the militia is the militant or the right wing, if you will, the front line, the hard line, of the patriot community. The patriot community is a broad spectrum... involving the militia all the way down to the Religious Right and the political action groups and jury reform legislative action groups."[3] Traditionally, citizen militias have been anti-government, anti-taxation and pro 2nd Amendment. Today, members of other right-wing, extremist groups, usually racially motivated, have joined the private militia movement, clouding the distinctive characteristics between the organizations. It has now become difficult to categorize the individual groups of the right-wing, because most of these organizations share many, fundamental beliefs, ranging from anti-gun control to hatred of all minorities. Throughout this analysis, I will focus on militias, but much of the research conducted has led to the conclusion that a crossover or merger of members within right-wing groups is occurring to some degree and will likely continue.

---

[2] James E. Duffy and Alan C. Brantley, M.A., "Militias: Initiating Contact," *FBI Law Enforcement Bulletin*, (July 1997): 4-6.

[3] Kenneth S. Stern, "Militias and the Religious Right," October 1996, *Institute for First Amendment Studies, Inc,.* URL: <http://www.ifas.org/fw/9610/militias html>. Downloaded 25 September 2000.

II   HISTORY

> *"Seemingly unnoticed, however, this variety of home-*
> *grown terrorist organizations had been emerging since*
> *the late 1970s. Although the spectacular antiwar, civil*
> *rights, and student movements of the 1960s and 1970s*
> *had dissipated, the 1980s saw the rise of some of the*
> *most spectacular and dangerous groups in U. S. history."*[4]
>
> *Brent L. Smith and Kelly R. Damphouse,*
> <u>*The Threat From Within*</u>

The militia movement in the United States is almost as old as the United States itself. At the very foundation of all militias, from 1786 to the present, there is likely to be a similar theme. Armed citizens organized into mobs (militias) to protest and possibly take action against what they consider to be an oppressive and tyrannical federal government. In 1786, the first major militia-style uprising occurred in colonial Massachusetts. Daniel Shay and a band of armed farmers, disgruntled over excess land taxation, organized to take action against the federal government. A few years after Shay's rebellion, in 1794, whiskey producers in Pennsylvania organized and armed themselves to protest against the excise tax placed on whiskey. The mass of armed citizens believed that the tax was an attack on their freedom as Americans and on their economic well-being: the Whiskey Rebellion. Militias, no matter what the year, their affiliation, or personal beliefs, base their views and patriotism on the image and lore of the militiamen during the period of the War for American Independence

---

[4]Brent L. Smith and Kelly R. Damphouse, "Two Decades of Terror: Characteristics, Trends, and Prospects for the Future of American Terrorism," in *The Future of Terrorism: Violence in the New Millennium,* ed. Harvey W. Kushner (London: Sage Publications, 1998), 133.

and shortly thereafter--ordinary men, who took up arms in an attempt to impose their will against an oppressive governmental system, a system that had become too large and exceedingly corrupt in their eyes.

John Birch, considered to be the direct ancestor of the modern militia movement, was a staunch opponent of big government and socialism. The John Birch Society, which bears his name, was founded in 1958, and attracted wealthy, young, well-educated men.[5] The Birch Society strongly opposed social security, income tax, welfare and civil rights. These ideas were seen as the work of communists working within the federal government; however, the Birch Society did not engage in terrorism or paramilitary operations. Their tactics were to write letters, issue propaganda and lobby. They had a large sympathetic audience in the U. S., but not many members.

In contrast to the non-violent Birch Society, Robert DePugh may be thought of as the founding father of the first modern day militia group that organized with paramilitary training at its core. Founded in 1961, his organization was called the Militiamen. DePugh was a former Birch Society member, but parted with the group due to an allegation of him trying to take over the Birch Society. He started his paramilitary training camp in California and advocated "If you're ever going to buy a gun, buy it now."[6] The movement never numbered more than a few hundred, but it was on the cutting edge. Some members had planned to assassinate then U. S. Senator J. William Fulbright, and release cyanide into the ventilation system of the United Nations building in New York City. In 1967, DePugh was arrested for violation of the

---

[5]Neil Hamilton, *Militias in America* (Santa Barbara, CA: ABC-CLIO, Inc, 1996), 12.

[6]Hamilton, 13.

National Firearms Act.[7]   That was the beginning of the end of the Militiamen

organization of DePugh, but the embers of the militia movement would burn on.

Because of large legal settlements against the traditional hate groups (the Ku

Klux Klan and Aryan Nations), membership enrollment declined in the 1990s;

whereas, privately organized militia groups and the membership therein soared.

Beginning in the late 1980s and early 1990s, "hate group" and militia watchdog

organizations, like the Southern Poverty Law Center (SPLC), the Anti Defamation

League (ADL), and the Montana Human Rights Network (MHRN), began winning

large settlements from traditional hate groups. In recent years, the Ku Klux Klan

organizations reportedly lost over 60 million dollars in assets, virtually wiping out

their financial base and causing bankruptcy, and the judgments won against the Aryan

Nations have led to the possible copyright loss of their organizational name and the

loss of their private compound in Hayden Lake, Idaho.[8]   Civil Rights attorney and co-

founder of the SPLC, Morris Dees, hoped that the 6.3 million dollar judgment won

against the Aryan Nations would be the beginning of the end of that white supremacist

sect.[9]   Because of the overt bigotry displayed by the traditional hate groups, their

recruiting pool was often limited to the "far-right". Subsequently, the legal

settlements against the "hate groups" have driven many of their members to either

seek out other organizations with shared beliefs or to establish their own

organizations.

---

[7]Hamilton, 13.

[8]"Attorney Morris Dees Pioneer in Using 'Damage Litigation' to Fight Hate Groups," *CNN*, 8 September 2000, *American On Line*, under the keyword "Dees," accessed 25 September 2000.

[9]"Attorney Morris Dees."

In October 1992, members of many far-right organizations and hate groups gathered in Estes Park, CO, at what they titled the "Rocky Mountain Rendezvous," to discuss the "wrongful" actions enacted upon Randy Weaver and his family at Ruby Ridge.[10] The intent of the representatives assembled, which included members of Christian Identity, Posse Comitatus, the Ku Klux Klan (KKK), the Aryan Nations, and numerous others, was not to reconcile their differences, but to put them aside and unite in principle, standing in unison for the causes they shared together.[11] Prior to this gathering, some groups even thought of the others as rivals, but the white supremacists, the tax resistors, 2nd Amendment advocates, anti-abortion extremists and anti-government proponents sympathized with each other and vowed to work together to fight the common enemy, **the U. S. government**. This was new to all in the extremist, right-wing, with the outcome being the formulation of citizen militias and the birth of the modern militia movement.

Today's notable militias include the Michigan Militia, Militia of Montana (MOM), Montana Unorganized Militias, Texas Emergency Reserve Militia, Posse Comitatus, and the Northern Michigan Regional Militia. At the end of the 1990s, at least one private militia trained and operated in each of the 50 states. Their names are well known and their information is wide spread. In the past, gun shows and local "survivalist expositions" accounted for the majority of the proliferation of militia information. However, with the advent of the WEB page, most militia information is

---

[10]Robert L. Snow, *The Threat From Within: Terrorists Among Us* (New York: Plenum Trade, 1999), 109-112.

[11]Morris Dees and James Corcoran, *Gathering Storm: America's Militia Threat* (New York: HarperCollins Publishing, 1996), 67.

now spread through the internet, a relatively cheap means of conveying their message, and accounting for the militias' continued development today. Of the six afore mentioned militias, all have or have had WEB sites posted on the internet.

III   BELIEFS AND IDEOLOGY

> *"Under the New World Order (NWO) private property rights and private gun ownership will be abolished, all national, state and local elections will become meaningless, the U. S. Constitution will be supplanted by the U. N. Charter, only **approved** churches and other places of worship will be permitted to operate and will become appendages of the One World Religion, home schooling will be outlawed and school curriculum will be approved by the U. N., and American military bases and other federal facilities will be used as concentration camps by the U. N. to confine patriots, including the militias, who defy the NWO."[12]*
>
> *Beliefs shared by patriots and extremist members of militias concerning the Y2K bug and the New World Order conspiracy theory.*

Militia members predominantly share the belief that the United States federal government is to blame for the demise of the American society. Robert Snow, author of The Militia Threat: Terrorists Among Us, states that the glue binding them together is a noxious compound of four ingredients: 1) an obsessive suspicion of the government; 2) a belief in anti-government conspiracy theories; 3) a deep-seated hatred of governmental officials; and 4) a feeling that the U. S. Constitution, for all intents and purposes, has been discarded by Washington bureaucrats.[13] Kenneth S.

Stern, author of Militias and the Religious Right, and A Force Upon the Plain: The

American Militia Movement and the Politics of Hate, adds that among the strongest

driving forces in the militia movement are racists and anti-Semites, including key

Christian Identity adherents, who seek to "Mainstream" their agenda through

opposition to gun control, federal regulations, environmental regulation, and to a

lesser extent, abortion in order to attract members.[14]

Historically, militias have attempted to keep the political process from dulling

their movement, or diluting their extremist tendencies with expression through ballot

or pen. Nevertheless, no matter what militia group referred to or if it is more or less

radical than the next, their hatred is directed at the U. S. government and their number

one concern is guns, then taxation, individual rights, education, etc. The right to bear

arms and gun "craze" philosophy is so deep-rooted within the militia movement that

the overwhelming belief is that U. S. government officials will one day knock on their

doors and seize their firearms. Several militia members interpreted the Brady Bill and

accompanying assault weapons ban in 1994 as just that, the precursors towards

disarming the common citizens within America in preparation for the "New World

Order" takeover, and that gun registrations would make it even easier for U. N. troops

to confiscate guns and arrest gun owners. This scenario was introduced in the 1978

novel, The Turner Diaries, written by William Pierce and commonly referred to as the

---

[12]Federal Bureau of Investigation, *Project Megiddo*: *An Analysis* (1999), 8. Cited hereafter as FBI, *Megiddo*.

[13]Snow, 26.

[14]Stern, "Militias and the Religious Right."

"bible" of the militia movement and right-wing extremism that details the U. N. sponsored takeover of the United States.[15]

Militia organizations commonly do not recognize any authority above the level of county government. This philosophy stems from the original citizen militias of the 18th century that were formed when the federal government was in its infancy, and when individual states wielded significant power. One such group, Posse Comitatus, believes that the Internal Revenue Service (IRS) has no legitimate power because the 16th amendment was never ratified and their authority to collect money is illegal. They likewise believe that the **enemy** (Jews) controls the federal government and they reject the legitimacy of the U. S. monetary system.[16]

On the issue of individual rights, the local sheriff of Waukesha, Wisconsin needed the assistance of a SWAT team in November 1998, to assist in the enforcement of a county ordinance, in the removal of junk and debris from the property of an anti-government activist. The activist threatened violence against anybody who tried to forcibly clean up his property.[17] Individuals who make up the militias share the thought that as long as they obey the laws in which they believe to be valid, than they should be able to do what they want, and when they want, especially on their own property.

In general, militia members resist paying income taxes, they advocate strict

---

[15]William Pierce, *The Turner Diaries* (Hillsboro, WV: Vanguard Books, 1978), 1-7.

[16]Harvey W. Kushner, Ph.D., *Terrorism in America* (Springfield, IL: Charles C. Thomas Publisher, Ltd., 1998), 64.

[17]"Calendar of Conspiracy: A Chronology of Anti-Government Extremist Criminal Activity" *The Militia Watchdog* 2, no. 4 (October-December 1998), <http://www.militia-watchdog.org/cocv2n4.htm>, accessed 15 January 2001.

adherence to 2nd Amendment rights and they firmly belief that the federal government is behind the formulation of the NWO, in which the United States will cease to exist as we know it and will give way to the mongrelization of one world society as directed by the United Nations. To illustrate this deep-seated belief and distrust of the United Nations, one right-wing extremist group planned to attack a celebration at Fort Hood, Texas, on July 4, 1997, in an attempt to engage U. N. troops they believed were there to begin the take over of the United States and start the "One World Government."[18] It is widely believed that U. N. forces, consisting of mostly foreign troops, will takeover the United States and impose martial law, while U. S. troops will go abroad and join in the takeover of the rest of the world to assist in establishing the One World Government. U. S. troops will be used abroad because they may have reservations about killing American citizens, whereas the foreign troops will not. This is by far their most skewed belief, which feeds their conviction of the "impending" armed conflict with the federal government that necessitates paramilitary training and the stockpiling of weapons in preparation.

However, there is a difference between the average militia member and the extremist. Average militia members are usually lower to middle-income white men worried about the economic security of their family, while long-term extremists tend to encourage the militia movement to more radical and violent tactics.[19] It is in the area of violence that the right-wing extremist movement offers a friendly breeding ground for psychologically imbalanced individuals who openly believe in the rhetoric

---

[18]Penny Owen, "FBI Says Dozens of Attacks Foiled," *The Daily Oklahoman*, 16 April 2000, 9A.

[19]Snow, 14.

calling for the destruction of the NWO. The OKC bombing appalled many militia members throughout the country, but Norm Olsen, the head of the Northern Michigan Regional Militia, stated that the victory achieved by the bombing of the Alfred P. Murrah federal building only cost them one soldier--McVeigh.[20] It is easy to conclude that the view of Norm Olsen may be still shared by many in the militia movement.

Some members in the militia movement and other right-wing organizations believed that Y2K would initiate the hostile takeover of the United Nations and were prepared to engage in military style warfare in an effort to thwart the attempt. In addition, others believed that the anticipated Y2K computer problems would lead to civilian disorder caused by the erroneous cessation of electrical, gas and water services. Individual militias would then be prepared to take over smaller, rural cities and reestablish infrastructure and civil order. In fact, fringe members in northern California were arrested for their role in actively plotting the destruction of public and private installations in an attempt to create enough chaos during the millennium activities that the President of the United States would declare martial law. This, they envisaged, would give the militia groups the opportunity to overthrow the government. Even smaller Y2K computer problems were likely to be perceived as part of a larger problem elsewhere within the U. S. infrastructure and had the potential to begin a panic within the militia communities. There were even members in particular militias who were trying to "turn a buck" by selling survivalist foods, products and literature. Their motto was, "Scare Em to Death and Then Sell Them Some Preparedness."[21]

---

[20]Snow, 103.

[21]Marc Cooper, "Y2K and the Militia: Whoopee, We're All Gonna Die...Rich!" *The Nation* 269, no. i6 (23 August 1999): 21.

13

Because the year 2000 came and went, the groups espousing the demise of the U. S. with relation to Y2K have subsided, but what are they up to now? Have they disarmed and disbanded? It is highly unlikely that they have disbanded because their belief in the corruption of the federal government is so strong that another opportunity will emerge for them to manipulate. When that opportunity arises, it will be enhanced through fabricated paranoia and exploited to achieve maximum hysteria through the cross section of American citizenry who shares their common beliefs. The acute paranoia of some militiamen, especially the radical fringe, have led them to believe that the federal government, so deeply involved with the conspiracy to take away the legal rights of Americans, committed the OKC bombing, spread toxins across America via contrails from aircraft, attempted to cause a drought and was responsible for the Sunset Limited train derailment on October 14, 1995 in Arizona. In reference to the OKC bombing and other terrorist activity, an unidentified member of the Texas Militia proclaimed, "Militias neither endorse this type of action, nor were involved; however, someone wanting it to appear otherwise was involved, and who or whom would that be?"[22]

IV   MEMBERSHIP

> *"Most observers of the modern militia movement find*
> *that, in stark contrast to the usually unemployed*
> *and often sociopathic individuals who make up America's*
> *most virulent hate groups, many members of the armed*
> *civilian militias hold jobs, have families, and have never*
> *been in trouble with the law."*[23]

---

[22]"Mystery Witness Sought in Amtrak Derailment," *CNN*, 14 October 1995, *America On Line*, under the keyword "Sunset Limited," accessed 10 January 2001.

[23]Snow, 14.

The modern definition of militias are "formal, structured, private organizations of armed citizens that declare themselves militias and engage in paramilitary training sessions or preparedness meetings, but without federal or state statute.[24] Members of militias come in all shapes and sizes, but the vast majority share common backgrounds. Most are white males, with limited educational backgrounds, in America's middle and working classes.

In the 1980s, Posse Comitatus and Aryan Nations, in an attempt to expand their membership roles, tried to rally the bewildered steel workers. Potential members found the anti-government rhetoric attractive, but the groups recruited very few new members because of their racial overtones.[25] In the hope of attracting new membership, Louis Beam, overt racist and leader of the Texas Emergency Reserve Militia, cut out his organizational racist theme and changed his rhetoric to only that of anti-government (over-regulation, over-taxing, strong 2nd Amendment rights, defeat the "New World Order"). He then was able to attract normal people who held normal jobs and whom were not in trouble with the law. The thousands who joined were just angry with the government, and woefully unaware of the deep-seated racial beliefs.[26]

Because a great portion of people in the militia movement have limited educations and cannot succeed in the modern workplace, they hold menial, low-paying

---

[24] Hamilton, 2.

[25] Dees and Corcoran, 2.

[26] Dees and Corcoran, 4.

jobs with little chance of advancement. They see more and more higher paying jobs in

the U. S. held by minorities, and they also see some of the traditionally higher paying

factory jobs leaving the country where cheaper labor exists. Consequently, they

cannot accept responsibility for their own personal and financial dilemmas, so they

turn toward a sympathetic cause--the militias, which in turn fuels the reasoning why

they are in such a lowly predicament and advises them on the actions to be taken in

response. However, specific events usually spark the largest surges in membership.

In the early 1990s, the two biggest events to stimulate the militia movement

were the Ruby Ridge siege of 1992, and the Branch Davidian incident in Waco, TX of

1993. In fact, the Missouri 51st Militia was so named in honor of the fifty-one day

standoff of the Branch Davidians.[27] Militia movement leaders believe that actions like

those taken in the eleven days at Ruby Ridge did more to increase their membership

roles than they could actively recruit in 20 years.[28] In 1999, the estimated number of

militia/"Patriot" groups operating within the United States was estimated at 217 and

hate groups at 457.[29] This number has fluctuated and the estimates have varied greatly

within the last seven years; however, the number of militia groups greatly increased in

1994 following the Waco and Ruby Ridge incidents, but decreased drastically after the

OKC bombing in 1995. Many attribute that decrease in membership to many

mainstream members not wanting to be affiliated with organizations whose rhetoric

included terrorist-style vengeance; however, the members who remain should be

---

[27]Snow, 101.

[28]Dees and Corcoran, 31.

[29]"Intelligence Report," Fall 2000, *Southern Poverty Law Center*, URL:
<http://www.splcenter.org/intelligenceproject/ip-mainbtm html>, accessed 19 February 2001.

considered dangerous and violent, because they almost certainly possess extremist and radical views.

Whether it be the FBI killing of Vicki and Samuel Weaver (wife and 14 year old son of Randy Weaver, respectively) at Ruby Ridge or the over aggressiveness of ATF agents at the Branch Davidian complex, mistakes, screw-ups and especially cover-ups by the federal government are the principle factors that aid in militia recruitment. People, who generally sympathize with the militia cause, are drawn into the movement when the government errs and militia spokespersons exploit the situation. In 1997 and 1998, the congressional hearings uncovering the corruption within the IRS served as another catalyst for the recruitment of members into the militia movement, further associating fraudulence with the federal government.

Also, militia leaders actively solicit military veterans or others with extensive expertise with firearms, explosives, and specialized training. Likewise, individuals may be attracted to militias for the chance to showcase their military abilities: Timothy McVeigh. Furthermore, it is not uncommon to discover that your local civil servant is a member of the local militia. Just two weeks after the bombing of the Alfred P. Murrah federal building in Oklahoma City, Indianapolis police sergeant James Heath shocked his fellow law enforcement brethren when an undercover video revealed that not only was he a member of the local militia, the Sovereign Patriots, but he was the leader. In addition, two weeks prior to the OKC bombing, the FBI sent a memo out to its field offices warning its agents to use caution, because it had received information

---

Information accessed 2 April 2001, via the same website, estimates an increase in the number of Hate Groups to 602 for 2000, but the number of "Patriot"/militia groups has not been updated.

that nationwide a number of local police officers had joined the ranks of civilian militias that held anti-government views.[30]

V   THE THREAT: PAST, PRESENT AND FUTURE! "REAL OR PERCEIVED"

"Assessing the magnitude of the threat posed by the militia groups operating today is a bit like gauging the risk to shipping posed by icebergs. The number that can be seen is important, but the real danger lies beneath the surface."[31]

Morris Dees of the
Southern Poverty Law Center

Domestic Terrorism, as defined by the FBI, is "the unlawful use, or threatened use, of force or violence by a group or individual based and operating entirely within the United States or Puerto Rico, without foreign direction, committed against persons or property to intimidate or coerce a government, the civilian population, or any segment thereof in furtherance of political or social objectives."[32] Based on the above definition, what militias espouse, teach, plan, and occasionally execute is <u>domestic terrorism</u>, but when did this new threat of domestic terrorism become associated with the militias?

---

[30]Snow, 58, 59.

[31]Snow, 231.

[32]*Terrorism in the United States: 1998*. Washington DC: Counterterrorism Threat Assessment and Warning Unit, National Security Division, Federal Bureau of Investigation, (undated, 1998).

It was neither the actions of Randy Weaver at Ruby Ridge, nor the actions of the Branch Davidians of Waco, but the actions of Timothy McVeigh that demonstrated the true threat of the militia movement in America. It was not until that event occurred that "threat awareness" was aroused in America about domestic terrorism and security around federal buildings throughout America increased to an unparalleled height. The security around most federal buildings today is higher than that around most military installations. Because militias and other right-wing organizations will not normally target military personnel, the threat of a militia attack on U. S. military personnel is far lower than the threat to other federal workers. Militia members believe that military personnel share their same warrior philosophy and ideals, even though military personnel are federal workers, per se.

With the potential to be the most horrendous incident since the OKC bombing, law enforcement officials in 1996 confiscated enough ricin (a deadly poison made from castor beans) to kill over 1400 people. Two members of the Minnesota Patriots allegedly manufactured the poison to use on government employees.[33] Also occurring in 1996, members of the Viper Militia of Arizona were arrested with over one ton of the same explosive material used in the OKC bombing. Viper militiamen were training other members in explosives handling, and actively scouting potential bombing targets. These members were definitely considered dangerous, and likewise, presented a threat to the general public. It is quite likely that only timely federal law

---

[33]Snow, 105, 106. Ricin is toxic by numerous exposure routes; however, its use by terrorists might involve poisoning of water or foodstuffs, inoculation via ricin-laced projectiles, or aerosolization of liquid ricin or lyophilized powder.

enforcement intervention kept another tragedy from occurring.[34] However, the difficult question is if the entire Viper militia organization is a threat? The answer is unclear and depends on one's individual perspective. The probability of an entire militia openly supporting and executing an incident of the magnitude of the OKC bombing is extremely small, but such actions by a few are highly probable. In an organization that cultivates hatred and distrust of the federal government, the possibility is strong that someone is fanatical enough to orchestrate a violent act. In 1995 alone, over 2,000 lbs of explosives were stolen from commercial job sites in five states.[35]

"In my 29 years of law enforcement, the militia movement has the possibility of developing into the greatest threat to the United States I've seen," stated Ex-ATF agent Steve Wortham.[36] "The real threat of the militias could be huge," said former ATF agent George Stoll in an interview. "It depends on how many of the lunatic fringe listen to the rhetoric, join up and then decide to do something."[37] These former law enforcement professionals fear the militia movement because of the possibility of armed citizens rising up against the U. S. government out of anger, fear, and paranoia. Dr. Mark Hamm, professor of criminology, Indiana State University, states that the overall threat that militias pose today is very different than in 1996; it has subsided

---

[34]Snow, 75.

[35]Dees and Corcoran, 210.

[36]Steve Wortham, interviewed by Robert L. Snow in *The Militia Threat: Terrorists Among Us*, 27. The date of the interview is unknown, but it is believed to have been conducted prior to 1998.

[37]George Stoll, interviewed by Robert L. Snow in *The Militia Threat: Terrorists Among Us*, 26. The date of the interview is unknown, but it is believed to have been conducted prior to 1998.

due to an increased threat awareness and effective dialogue between law enforcement agencies and militias, but he adds that the radical fringe (which he estimates at 15,000 nationwide) is as big a threat today as it ever was--unpredictable, paranoid and not going away. He maintains that the radical fringe violence will continue, but hopefully not to the degree that Timothy McVeigh chose, although possible.[38] Realistically, not since the Civil War has the potential existed for so many citizens, individually or collectively, to take up arms in anger against this country. Why is this? Some of this can be attributed to globalization, the North American Free Trade Agreement (NAFTA) and immigrant workers, any measure that has taken good paying, low-skilled jobs away from Americans. The increase of minorities in the higher paying jobs and in the higher echelons of American society are other reasons. Is this threat of attack from militias real, or perceived? According to the investigation that ensued after the OKC bombing of April 19, 1995, Timothy McVeigh was not affiliated with any militia or Patriot group, but merely a fringe member who twisted "militia justice" and took it a dangerous step further. He certainly possessed beliefs shared by many in the militia movement, but it was McVeigh's desire for vengeance for the federal government's role in the Waco incident that provided him the impetus to act, and his personal copy of The Turner Diaries that gave him the architecture to execute the bombing of the Alfred P. Murrah federal building. In addition to The Turner Diaries promoting the destruction of a federal building and illustrating the ensuing armed conflict between "The Organization" (militias and other extremist right-wing groups)

---

[38]Mark R. Hamm, PhD., Professor of Criminology, Indiana State University, telephone interview by the author, 20 February 2001. Dr. Hamm is the author of several books regarding militias and hate groups.

and the United States government, it advocates the annihilation of blacks and Jews. A truly disturbing fact is that these diaries are not the only publication available to give advice to the few in the American public who want to commit violence in behalf of the militia movement. Recently posted on the <u>Militia of Montana Online Information Center</u> was the following advertisement: *"**BANNED BOOKS:** The U. S. Senate is out to make the distribution and sale of any book or other material that instructs an individual on how to make an explosive device illegal. Go here for some great deals on these soon to be ILLEGAL items. GET YOUR COPIES TODAY!"*[39]

According to Morris Dees, the threat that militias in the United States present is not enough to start a **revolution** because they do not possess the power to do so, but they certainly have the power to hurt a lot of people.[40] Nonetheless, some of the same extremist rhetoric spoken by Norm Olsen, Louis Beam, and others regarding potential terrorist actions can be found in the book, <u>Urban Guerrilla Minimanual</u>, written by the late Brazilian urban guerrilla, Carlos Marighella, about revolution and how to arm for one. In reality, many in the militia movement do not believe in these strong practices of terrorist-style violence, and most in law enforcement believe that only the fringe fanatics actually espouse and conduct radical violence and the danger is not widespread, but isolated and limited. But the modern militia movement has made it more difficult for federal law enforcement agencies to investigate their illegal actions. Since most counter terrorism investigations have centered on terrorist groups, the

---

[39]"Militia of Montana Online Information Center," *Militia of Montana*, URL: <http://www.militiaofmontana.com>, accessed 16 November 2000.

[40]Snow, 91. The statements provided by Morris Dees are undated in the text, but they are believed to have been made prior to 1998.

majority of militias operating within the United States today are organized into <u>small cells</u>, which are characterized as <u>leaderless and autonomous</u>, and outside of the public eye. Some militias organize, train, and execute violence "underground", and have begun to restrict their membership to only the most ultra right-wing recruits. While the leader of any particular militia may not openly support or encourage acts of violence, it is easy to understand how these small cells of members or splinter groups take part in violent acts without the knowledge of the leader. These individuals are affiliated with the groups, carry the name of the organization, but may perpetuate acts of violence of their own.[41] There is no telling how many militias are conducting operations this way and what their true intentions are. Author Ken Kreps states that the Montana Unorganized Militias are a loose collection of Montana citizens preparing to defend Americans from all possible tyranny. Many of their "Assault" units are **allegedly** available 24 hours a day to respond to crimes against the people.[42] The problem with monitoring and reporting on the threat of the "underground" militias is the lack of verifiable and substantial information.

Is there still a significant threat for the 21st century? In July 2000, a Golden, Colorado man was indicted for allegedly manufacturing numerous explosive devices and selling them to undercover agents. The investigation began after the man hosted a two-day paramilitary course in Park County, CO for several militia groups. Although the strength of each device was the equivalent of a quarter stick of dynamite, and not

---

[41]FBI, *Megiddo*, 16.

[42]Ken Kreps, "Militias-Armed and Deadly," 28 September 2000, *Themestream*, URL: <http://www.themestream.com/gspd>, accessed 6 November 2000. Unable to confirm report of Montana Unorganized Militias assault units to respond 24 hours a day, seven days a week.

very powerful, local law enforcement officials were not taking any chances with the events of the Columbine High School massacre and the OKC bombing still fresh on the minds of many. [43] County officials in Everett, WA must think the threat was still serious in October 2000, because the U. S. Department of Justice issued Snohomish County $100,000 to purchase equipment to deal with the threat and aftermath of a terrorist attack. [44] It must be remembered that the states, which make up the northwest United States, are a hotbed for militia activity, and white supremacists have moved to the Northwest because they know there are others with similar sentiments and that resistance to their ideology is low in many of the communities. Too many Northwest residents tolerate white supremacy groups in their midst, either because they do not know how to respond or they are apathetic. [45] The ultimate goal of the Aryan Nations is to forcibly take five northwestern states--Oregon, Idaho, Washington, Montana and Wyoming--from the United States government in order to establish an Aryan Homeland, because, east of the Cascade Mountains, these states have limited African-American, Asian and Jewish populations, a prerequisite for starting their "whites only" area. [46]

Notwithstanding the rhetoric and motives of the extremist right-wing, Special Agent (SA) Steven Berry, FBI Public Affairs for Terrorism and National Security,

---

[43]Kevin Flynn, "Two Men Indicted in Explosives Inquiry: One-time Militia Leader, Businessman Accused of Selling Devices to Agents," *Denver Rocky Mountain News*, 22 July 2000, 6A.

[44]Kate Reardon, "County Prepares for Possible Terrorism," *Daily Herald*, Everett (WA), 27 October 2000.

[45]Erin Walter, "Militias Want Destruction, Not Reform," *Lewiston Morning Tribune* (ID), 11 December 1999.

[46]FBI, *Megiddo*, 16.

states that militia violence is on the decline.[47] Indeed, over the past two years, the vast

majority of evidence supports this conclusion. Only modest terrorist activity was

reported or investigated during 2000 regarding American citizen militias; although,

numerous members of militias were either brought to trial or convicted for past crimes

in 2000. Nevertheless, one does not have to look too far in the past to find active

investigations and arrests of either militia members or radical fringe members who

were involved in domestic terrorist activities. Terrorism in the United States-1998, the

most current FBI periodical available regarding the subject, listed twelve potential acts

of terrorism as prevented in the United States that year. Nine of these acts were being

planned by American, right-wing extremists. In February 1998, FBI agents arrested

Larry Wayne Harris, a microbiologist and former member of Aryan Nations and his

co-conspirator, William Leavitt, Jr., for possessing the deadly biological agent

anthrax. Harris boasted, although incorrectly, that they had enough of the agent to

wipe out the city of Las Vegas. [48]

In another arena, extremist, right-wing organizations are increasingly taking up

the cause of abortion. The new tactics committed by anti-abortion activists are

performed by "leaderless cells" and common law courts, initiating fraudulent charges

against the doctors who perform abortions. In general, the number of common law

courts in the United States has dramatically increased. Many in the right-wing

movement no longer recognize or believe in the American justice system; therefore,

---

[47]Special Agent Steven W. Berry, FBI Public Affairs specializing in Terrorism and National Security Issues, telephone interview by the author, 3 January 2001.

[48]Louis R. Mizell, Jr., *Target USA* (New York: John Wiley and Son, Inc, 1998), 200.

common law courts are just another way to justify anti-government, anti-abortion, anti-Semitic, and other extremist feelings. In 1999, Matthew Trewhella, notorious anti-choice activist and member of the National Constitution Party, spoke out recently, after signing a declaration stating that murdering abortion providers is "justifiable" homicide, saying, "This Christmas I want you to do the most loving thing and I want you to buy each of your children an SKS assault rifle and 500 rounds of ammunition."[49] John Trochmann of MOM tells his members to arm themselves for the 2nd American Revolution by possessing an AR-15 semi-automatic assault rifle, 600 rounds of .233 ammunition and encourages them to read books on guerrilla warfare, special forces operations and sniper training.[50]

Author William Diehl, the personal photographer for Martin Luther King, Jr. and the only Caucasian in the late civil rights leader's entourage, stated in 1998, "I was shocked at how volatile the situation is." "One day soon, one of these groups is going to declare war."[51] Disregarding the militias just yet is not an option. While in recent years, militia groups and overall membership have declined, federal law enforcement agencies and private watchdog organizations expect to be monitoring militia groups and other right-wing extremist organizations well into the future.

---

[49]"Extremist Right-Wing Ideas Find Another Outlet," *Montana Human Rights Network*, May 2000, URL: <http://www.mhrn.org>, accessed 16 November 2000.

[50]Dees and Corcoran, 82.

[51]"Militia Terror," *Maclean's* 111, no. 3 (19 January 1998): 62.

VI   TRENDS

"I am following God's law. Blacks, Jews are welcome.
But when America is the new Israel, they'll need to go
back where they came from. It's just nature's law--kind
should go unto kind."[52]

John Trochmann,
leader of the Militia of Montana

Even as the 20th century ended with militia membership on the decline, the estimated number of members nationwide was in the tens of thousands, with the number of sympathizers in the millions. If the roles of militia groups stay intact, the armed civilian militia would still be an extremely powerful voice in smaller communities and a dangerous force in this country for the 21st century.[53] Indeed, the vast majority of militias are located in rural, small town USA, where militia seeds are easily sewn and cultivated, and large areas of sparsely populated land exist which aid in concealing their paramilitary training.

With militias finding a "sympathetic" ear in some small towns, or at least no strong opposition to their agenda, militia members could become the highly vocal majority in many small cities throughout rural America. Even without a majority voice in politics, militia members have infiltrated numerous town meetings throughout

---

[52]Snow, 113.

[53]Snow, 70.

27

the northwest United States in an attempt to disrupt, intimidate and enforce their opinions on local governments.[54]

> At a public meeting held in Everett, WA in 1996, by the local Democratic Party, officials from the Northwest Coalition Against Malicious Harassment and the Coalition for Human Dignity spoke out about white supremacy, Christian Patriotism and the militias. During the meeting, 30 members of the Washington State militia burst into the peaceful assembly to disrupt and intimidate the audience and speakers.[55] Likewise, at a township meeting in Wellston, MI, a militia member stood up and threatened to forcibly remove the presiding official from the room for having an opinion counter to that of the militia member.[56]

Concerning paramilitary training, ATF undercover agents reported that the Viper Militia conducted two types of training sessions involving the shooting of firearms. "A-shoots" were conducted with members bringing only legal weapons and open to family members and friends to observe and participate; for "B-shoots", only militia members could attend because explosives training and illegal automatic weapons firing were carried out.[57] Evidence supports that militias, or at least small cells of members within militias, can be considered dangerous, because of their beliefs, their training, and their actions.

Another alarming realization is that many factions of the extremist right-wing are agreed on in ideology, have "cross over" members, and have attempted a measure of cooperation. One of the main reasons for the intermingling of ideologies is that the

---

[54]Paul de Armond, "Militias and CLUE Activity in Whatcom and Snohomish Counties," 1996, *Militia Chronology*, URL: <http://nwcitizen.com/publicgood/reports/militiachron html>, accessed 2 April 2001.

[55]Armond.

[56]Snow, 225.

[57]Snow, 72.

more extremist militia leaders now appearing on the scene have backgrounds from the traditional hate groups (Aryan Nations, KKK, neo-Nazi groups, etc), and other racial, religious and ethnic hate groups.[58] Additionally, other groups, such as Posse Comitatus, have always espoused a wide range of beliefs and opinions. Posse Comitatus, who embraces a fundamentalist belief in the U. S. Constitution, and rejects nearly all post-Civil War amendments, refers to whites as independent "sovereign citizens" who need not comply with most modern legislation, particularly taxes; another indication that some in the anti-government regime possess white supremacist views.[59] Phineas Priests, another ultra-extremist, gun toting, loosely configured grouping, could be categorized as a militia or a religious order, but definitely racist.

Over the past few years, more and more white supremacist groups have strategically crossed over members into militias with the intent of concealing their identity, without overtly advertising their racist views. Consequently, in the two-year period between 1995 and 1997, militia membership outnumbered that of the KKK, the neo-Nazis, and the racist Skinheads combined.[60] Furthermore, with the inclusion of white supremacists in the militia movement, the overt racist rhetoric of these new members has subsided or disappeared; however, the feelings are still very present, but hidden underneath. Some white supremacists have crossed back over into the traditional hate groups because the majority of the militias were found to be too benign to house such extremist views. From the racially inspired church of the

---

[58]"Militias-Armed And Deadly."

[59]Brian Levin, "The Patriot Movement, Past, Present and Future," in *The Future of Terrorism: Violence in the New Millennium*, ed. Harvey W. Kushner (London: Sage Publications, 1998), 106.

[60]Snow, 112.

Christian Identity to the militias, it is highly probable for a person to be a member of more than one group or to move from one group to another. For the disenchanted, if a member of one group believes that group to be lax in its convictions, he or she will gravitate to a group that is more radical, or begin a group on their own. Michael Fortier, convicted in the OKC bombing for not informing officials of McVeigh's intent, stated at McVeigh's trial that he (McVeigh) wanted to start a militia group while living in Arizona in 1994, but he could not find enough people who thought and felt as militant as he did.[61]

While open hate of minorities is not what most militias are all about, some have tolerated and even welcomed racist crossover elements into their ranks. These must be considered high in their potential for irrational behavior, coupled with the mix of arms and explosives.

Dr. Hamm believes that it is only the radical and ultra-extremist militias that are racist and crossing over the white supremacists and Christian Identity types.[62]

> "In 2001, the majority of militias are mainstream and at one end of the continuum, while the militias which give favor to the "Louis Beams" of the world are at the other end. Louis Beam represents the radical fringe and where he is found, radical followers, racist-borne militias and other ultra-extremist organizations will proliferate; you will also find that your mainstream militias vehemently dislike the "Louis Beams" and "Timothy McVeighs" types because terrorist-style violence and racism are not the messages that they want to spread."[63]

---

[61] Snow, 103.

[62] Hamm telephone interview.

[63] Hamm telephone interview.

But what if militias should coalesce? Is it a possibility? And if so, what then? In some respects, groups within the extremist right-wing are coalescing, yet not achieving the in-depth, unity of effort needed to be a viable threat.

With the cross-pollination of members between the different right-wing organizations, comes an inherent level of cooperation. This essentially makes the efforts of the law enforcement agencies more difficult as there are no distinctive borders between groups and ideology.[64] However, the real danger of open coalescing and cooperation that the participants of the Rocky Mountain Rendezvous yearned for never materialized. As cited in chapter four, the Ruby Ridge incident of 1992 not only increased membership, but also was another in a series of events that caused militias and other right-wing organizations to band together and fight a unified battle. One chief conclusion which emerged from the Rocky Mountain Rendezvous in 1992, convened two months after Ruby Ridge, was that in order for militias and other organizations to increase membership and attain societal approval, the movements would need to tone down the racist and anti-Semitic rhetoric and concentrate on the anti-government theme in which acceptance could be found; however, cooperation between the militias and amongst the other extremist right-wing organizations has not led to any long term alliances or coalescing. SA Berry is not particularly worried about the coalescing of militias or the perceived dangers thereof. At this time, the indicators are not present, and for the foreseeable future, the militias are too loosely organized to promote that level of unity, he notes.[65] Americans should not worry

---

[64]FBI, *Megiddo*, 16.

[65]Berry telephone interview.

about the right-wing uprising as portrayed in The Turner Diaries. In fact, **if** the militias and other extremist right-wing groups wanted to launch a revolution within the United States, it would require three ingredients: 1) **one** very charismatic leader, 2) a level of cooperation within the different right-wing organizations that has never been able to materialize because of too many disparate beliefs, many of which are too extremist or violent to rate a significant following, and 3) a country weakened through economic, societal, cultural and moral losses, much to the likeness of post-World War I Germany.

Today, the majority of the public views militias as nothing more than a breeding ground for fanatics capable of the same destruction as in OKC, who share the same bizarre conspiracy theories and anti-government beliefs. This belief was amplified in the past by the MOM openly selling a militia manual that gave training guidance in the areas of kidnapping and execution of governmental officials, raiding armories for weapons and the bombing of federal and private installations.[66] Although few members of militias initially foresaw the devastating incident that would occur in OKC, the probability of copycat crimes is still high in the years that have followed. Even with the vast majority of domestic terrorist incidents committed by the radical fringe or splinter organizations within the militia movement, the number of militias and other extremist groups is still sizeable, and the members are involved in a variety of criminal and "bogus" activities.

---

[66]Snow, 103. The manual, entitled M. O. D. Training Manual, appears not to have been written by any members of MOM, and allegedly, no members of MOM can remember what M. O. D. was an abbreviation for.

Some members have started financing their militia activities by producing and selling drugs; marijuana and methamphetamines seem to be the most popular. Other traditional and more dangerous activities to raise funds have always included bank robberies and armored car heists. Members feel that criminal deeds to advance their cause is to be tolerated because it does not harm them directly, but it does aid them financially in the continuance of their struggle. In addition to criminal activity, one by-product of the militia movement is the concept of "common law" courts. These perverse and bogus courts obviously have no legal authority, but they have been created by the militias and other right-wing organizations to not only adjudicate their internal problems, but more importantly, to exonerate the militia members of their pending legal problems in the nation's bonafide court system. Frequently, these common law courts have even issued fraudulent warrants and subpoenas to local, state and federal officials who the common law courts alleged were guilty of conspiracy and corruption.

Some right-wingers have actively sought involvement in the political process: David Duke, outspoken racist and former Klan wizard, was an unsuccessful candidate for governor of Louisiana. Numerous congressional members during the 1990s openly sympathized with or were former members of militias and other extremist right-wing groups. The most notable member was Idaho Representative Helen Chenoweth, former Georgia Klansperson, initially elected to congress in 1994.

> Fortunately, neither Congresswoman Chenoweth nor any
> other militia advocates in congress had enough power or influence
> to push through resolutions or bills favoring the militia movement,
> or the power to make the militias a huge force in this country. Yet
> the support these politicians give to what are basically private armies,
> and the shared belief of these politicians in many of the wild and

baseless conspiracy theories espoused by the militia, should be a frightening wake-up call to the American public.[67]

In fact, their paramilitary activities notwithstanding, the Michigan Militia can be seen at times to perform functions similar to those of conventional pressure groups or political parties.[68] When a militia organization displays this type of political behavior, two things are apt to happen. First, the militia will gain substantial credibility and legitimacy within the public eye. That particular militia, or grouping of militias will become more mainstream, gain additional mainstream membership, and begin to introduce their issues into the political process. However, whether real or just well hidden, some of the "hardline" rhetoric will have to be subdued to accommodate the new constituents, and the open "paramilitary" style of operations may begin to wane. Secondly, this is usually the point where the true radicals tend to distance themselves or totally separate from that particular militia and seek another more violent and extremist venue. In either case and at the present time, the current U. S. political environment does not mix with the common militia ideology, especially when the typical militia infrastructure is centered around paramilitary operations.

While it may be true that within recent years international terrorism in the United States may be on the decline, all evidence indicates that domestic terrorism planned, attempted or committed by right-wing groups is still a viable threat and will continue, albeit hopefully without the severity of the OKC bombing.

---

[67]Snow, 174.

[68]Mariani, 132.

VII   LAW ENFORCEMENT AND PRIVATE EFFORTS

> *"If militia people are killed by federals, roughly 1.5 million armed, uniformed militia are in training and ready. It could reverberate across the country in a firestorm."*[69]
>
> *Norm Olsen, leader of the Northern Michigan Regional Militia, of the Freemen standoff at Justus Township, Montana.*

Prior to the OKC bombing of 1995, the FBI had fewer than 100 investigations open concerning domestic terrorism, as compared to over 900 investigations pending by the end of 1997.[70] Since the OKC bombing, aggressive law enforcement actions, consisting of "beefed up" intelligence, paid informants, and an open dialogue between militias and law enforcement agencies, have significantly reduced the threat of radical militia violence. In addition, one year after the OKC bombing, anti-terrorism legislation gave the FBI an additional $370 million to hire nearly 2000 agents and build up its counter terrorism program. The FBI stated that its investigations of potential terrorism have increased nearly tenfold since then.[71] It is not clear how many of the current investigations are attributed to international or domestic terrorists, but it

---

[69]Snow, 215.

[70]David E. Kaplan and Mike Tharp, "Terrorism Threats at Home: Two Years After Oklahoma City, Violent Sects Abound," *U. S. News and World Report* 123, no, 25 (29 December 1997): 22.

[71]Owen, "FBI says," 9A.

is interesting to note that the investigations have chiefly focused on domestic terrorism and the actions of right-wing organizations.

Most evidence points to only radical individuals as the perpetrators who plan and commit terrorist acts, but overwhelmingly, these same individuals once found favor and refuge in the militias and camaraderie among the other members. In general, it is the radicals that the FBI focuses their investigations on and not an entire militia group. According to SA Berry, the FBI does not investigate militia groups or any other organization as a whole; they only investigate individuals.[72] Furthermore, as long as no unlawful acts are committed or threatening behavior indicated, then there is nothing technically illegal about forming a militia. In fact, the U. S. Constitution, as presently interpreted, prohibits the FBI from scrutinizing any group of lawfully assembled citizens.[73] Thus, the FBI cannot and will not start an investigation until there is credible evidence that an individual or a group of individuals is actively planning an act of domestic terrorism. However, in a great number of cases, when federal weapons violations are committed, and open threats to individuals and/or facilities are planned, then law enforcement officials must step in and take action. The most popular cause for law enforcement officials to initiate an investigation is through possession of illegal weapons.[74]

---

[72] Berry telephone interview. In a re-interview conducted on 3 April 2001, SA Berry states that the FBI does not seek to estimate the number of Hate Groups or Militia Organizations because that could be considered infringing on their civil rights, since the groups are legal. SA Berry further stated that, in general, the FBI relies on the SPLC and other "watchdog" agencies to produce the annual estimates.

[73] Richard Ruelas, "FBI Agent: Arizona Hotbed of Militias," *The Arizona Republic* (Phoenix), 24 January 1999, A15.

[74] Berry telephone interview.

A relatively new tactic in the fight against right-wing terrorism in America that has paid off for the FBI has been to open the lines of communication with members of militia groups. After the OKC bombing, FBI Director Louis Freeh ordered top field agents to meet with established militia groups around the country, hoping to open doors and defuse tension. By initiating dialogue, many misperceptions which militias believed about the FBI, or other law enforcement agencies have been set aside, and vice versa. The leaders of one prominent group, the Michigan Militia Corps, tipped off the bureau about Brendon Blasz, a local activist who allegedly spoke of bombing government offices, federal armories and a Kalamazoo TV station.[75]

In addition, the FBI, ATF and other law enforcement agencies learned valuable lessons from the Ruby Ridge and Branch Davidian calamities. When, in 1996, it came time for a show down with the "Freemen" of *Justus Township*, Montana, federal officials decided not to make the same mistake thrice. The FBI negotiated with the Freemen through an eighty-one day standoff that sorely tested the FBI's resolve never to repeat the disasters of Ruby Ridge or Waco again. The FBI spent millions of dollars during the negotiations with the Freemen, but no blood was shed on either side and the standoff ended peacefully. It is highly likely that the actions taken by the FBI, during the Freemen standoff, saved America from a whirlwind of future militia violence. "A violent end to this standoff would have only reconfirmed the militia's belief in a brutal, corrupt government, and would have dashed forever any hopes of every convincing the more moderate militia sympathizers that the federal government

---

[75]Kaplan and Tharp, 22.

could be an entity that has the best interests of the people at heart."[76] In fact, Timothy McVeigh claimed that the OKC bombing was in response to the injustice and brutal treatment of the Branch Davidians in Waco, TX. Law enforcement agencies responsible for conducting investigations and making arrests within the militia movement must always be "above board" with evidentiary and enforcement procedures. At a minimum, this must be adhered to by all federal and local law enforcement agencies. When the American public perceives an impropriety of any federal agency and a cover up or scandal ensues, militia recruiting will increase and violent behavior within the militias will likely result. The recent problems of the IRS are perfect examples that served as catalysts to drive American citizens into the militia movement, one more tangible and unarguable illustration that signifies that portions of the federal government are corrupt. Could it be possible that an armed group would want law enforcement officials to overreact during a confrontation and initiate harsh measures or a "bloodbath"? Yes, the radical fringe wanted to set in motion this scenario during the Y2K hysteria, which, in turn, would have initiated marshal law in the U. S. to their benefit. Another occasion could be on the horizon; whether it be the handling of an investigation of militia members gone bad, or the outright abuse of power of any law enforcement agency, anything to deny legitimacy to the federal government and raise awareness to governmental corruption in general will further the militia cause.

Outside organizations have aided in the efforts of local and federal law enforcement agencies. **Watchdog** organizations (SPLC, MHRN, etc.) do a great job

---

[76]Snow, 218.

explaining and illustrating hatred. In numerous cases, the information that law enforcement agencies receive is from watchdog organizations. The SPLC and others are non-profit organizations and receive financial contributions through individual contributors; therefore, some of these private groups are influenced by personal agenda and ego: skewed—sure, but positive and overall, vital![77] In fact it was the SPLC, who sent a letter to the Justice Department in 1994, informing them of the growing threat of violence from some militia groups; the OKC bombing underscored the danger that the SPLC had foreseen.[78]

VIII   SPECULATION AND ANALYSIS

"During the year 2000 and beyond, the Turner Diaries *will be an inspiration for right-wing terrorist groups to act because it outlines both a revolutionary takeover of the government and a race war. These elements of the book appeal to a majority of right-wing extremists because it is their belief that one or both events will coincide with the new millennium."[79]*

Excerpt from Project MEGIDDO, an FBI strategic assessment of the potential for domestic terrorism in the United States undertaken in anticipation of the new millennium.

---

[77]Hamm telephone interview.

[78]Snow, 229.

[79]FBI, *Megiddo*, 8.

In 1995, few imagined that an individual or small group of Americans would ever attempt to kill a large group of innocent men, women and children. Could this happen again? The resounding answer is yes. Will it ever happen again? Recent analysis illustrates that even the extremist tendencies of individuals within militias or the radical fringe seem to be declining, and SA Berry believes the decline will continue, especially since the hype of the Y2K/millennium devastation has subsided, although not without the help of law enforcement. But there is widespread speculation about the recent legal motions of Timothy McVeigh, regarding his decision to end all legal challenges and appeals concerning his subsequent execution and to have his execution date expedited.[80] Since the militia movement is stimulated by martyrs, it is highly probable that Timothy McVeigh will become a martyr to those who share his beliefs. However, will McVeigh's execution date impact others in the same way that the Waco anniversary date impacted McVeigh? The answer is unclear, but there is little fear of the potential for Timothy McVeigh's execution date to stir up a militia uprising within the United States, but sporadic radical violence is very possible.

In the end, McVeigh's execution date may not hold any significance at all within the militia movement or even within the fringes; however, special days in the mythology of the terrorist subculture hold fundamental and philosophical meaning, and law enforcement officials should not ignore them. It is highly probable that law enforcement agencies nationwide will be on heightened alert on the actual day and

---

[80]"Convicted Oklahoma City Bomber Timothy McVeigh, on Federal Death Row for the Deadliest Act of Terrorism in U. S. History, Wants to Stop His Court Appeals and Ask the President for Clemency," *MSNBC*, 13 December 2000, *MSN.COM*, under the keywords "McVeigh", accessed on 24 December 2000.

anniversary dates that follow. Whether it be from militias or the radical fringe, SA

Berry would not speculate on the potential for right wing, domestic terrorism in

conjunction with the day of McVeigh's execution or on the follow-on anniversary

dates,[81] but Deputy Marshall Tom Davis of the U. S. Marshal's Service stated that he

will be on a heightened state of alert.[82] However, a person does not have to be

deceased to be a hero to militia followers. At a gun show in Springfield, MO in

January 2000, numerous people came to meet Randy Weaver, perpetrator of the Ruby

Ridge siege (or its victim, to Weaver supporters). There, Weaver signed copies of his

new book, The Federal Siege At Ruby Ridge.[83] It appears that the members of society

who were sympathetic to Weaver's cause have a good memory.

These fanatics will strike again. Why, because there are still scores of issues in

American politics and society that will excite them enough to act. As long as they are

armed, exhibit violent behavioral characteristics, and possess the paramilitary know-

how, citizens and facilities will continue to be targeted and the potential for Americans

to die will continue to exist. In 1998, Mark Hamm painted a frightful picture

pertaining to the future of domestic terrorism, especially attacks on federal

---

[81]Berry telephone interview. It is the opinion of the author that McVeigh's execution will have profound significance within the Extremist Right-Wing. While the American culture does support martyrs and heroes, he (McVeigh) will be not be a martyr to millions of Americans, but he will certainly be to those of his kind.

[82]Tom Davis, Deputy Marshal, U. S. Marshal Service, telephone interview by author, 12 January 2001. Davis states that the federal officials whom he guards in the Chicago area are still subject to militia and radical extremist threats.

[83]Donna Barton, "Ruby Ridge Survivor Draws Crowd to Gun, Knife Show," The News Leader (Springfield, MO), 31 January 2000.

judges and law enforcement officials.[84] His belief is that no one can ever predict the actions of the radical element that makes up portions of the militia movement; however, he is certain that the radical fringe will continue to strike again and again.[85]

IX   CONCLUSION

With the militia movement representing only a small fraction of the American public, who are mostly middle class, middle-aged, white males, the movement generally holds little national legitimacy, and the threat to national security is **assessed** as low. However, with the suspected operation of "leaderless resistance cells," "underground", and "unorganized" activity, the true threat or intent is unclear, and the threat awareness of the general public is low. However, the radical fringe that follows the militia movement commits the vast majority of domestic terrorism within the United States. These open acts of violence committed by the radical fringe will fluctuate based on the real or perceived corruption and abuse of power within the federal government, particularly focusing on the actions taken by federal law enforcement agencies. The radical fringe is made up of calculated, intelligent and cold individuals, sometimes formed into small cells, who possess a different set of societal

---

[84]Mark R. Hamm, PhD, "Terrorism, Hate Crime, and Antigovernment Research: A Review of the Research," in *The Future of Terrorism: Violence in the New Millennium*, ed. Harvey W. Kushner (London: Sage Publications, 1998), 56.

[85]Hamm telephone interview.

and cultural values. These different values, coupled with their obsession, cause them to commit violence against their fellow Americans.

Each perceived act of corruption or abuse of power committed by the federal government is just another forewarning of the impending takeover of the New World Order in the minds of militia members. Primarily, their hatred and suspicion of the U. S. government extends from their belief in the New World Order prophecy detailed in The Turner Diaries, which is fueled by their general opposition to government itself, gun control, taxation and the authority of the federal government to encroach upon their *perceived* individual rights, adding to the reasons why the majority of militia members view all government above the level of county as unjust, corrupt, tyrannical and not **of** the people.

Generally, the militia movement is not predisposed to committing large-scale violence to achieve their goals, so for the federal government to be effective in limiting the existing threat, the open dialogue between militia groups and law enforcement agencies must continue, and law enforcement agencies must remain approachable. Some in the American public will agree with portions of the militia rhetoric pertaining to gun control and taxation, adding to militia legitimacy, but in general, the militia and right-wing extremist rhetoric is too militant for mainstream America. The threat of the militia movement to national security will remain low as long as militias achieve no level of coalescing and their "hardline" message, which offends most Americans, stays constant.

However, for militias to gain support within the American public, the movement merely needs to display governmental corruption, deny U. S. governmental legitimacy by presenting federal misuse or excessive use of power to the public, and demonstrate the federal government's eagerness to encroach upon the individual rights of their members and society in general. In addition, to gain widespread acceptance, militias must be seen as organizations much more diverse than their present ranks exhibit. The organizations cannot be seen as a movement appealing only to middle class, middle-aged, white males living mostly in the sparsely populated areas of the Midwest and northwest United States. The movement must separate from the right-wing extremist philosophy (racism, bigotry, Christian purity) in order to gain political influence and representation at the national level.

Militia and right-wing extremist activity no longer airs on the evening news, but the threat is still present, waiting for an opportunity to arise; for it takes only one incident to be mishandled or covered up by federal government agencies to ignite a militia or right-wing extremist uproar in the United States. Subsequently, federal officials and law enforcement agents are most at risk from militia and right-wing extremist violence when it does occur, but the "collateral damage" can be spread over a wide path and affect hundreds.

BIBLIOGRAPHY

Interviews

Berry, Steven W., Special Agent. FBI Public Affairs specializing in Terrorism and National Security Issues. Telephone interview by the author, 3 January 2001.

Davis, Tom, Deputy Marshal. U. S. Marshal Service. Telephone interview by author, 12 January 2001.

Hamm, Mark R. PhD. Professor of Criminology, Indiana State University. Telephone interview by the author, 20 February 2001.

Stoll, George. Interviewed by Robert L. Snow. In *The Militia Threat: Terrorists Among Us.* Interview date unknown.

Steve Wortham. Interviewed by Robert L. Snow. In *The Militia Threat: Terrorists Among Us.* Interview date unknown.

Books

Dees, Morris, and James Corcoran. *Gathering Storm: America's Militia Threat.* New York: HarperCollins Publishing, 1996.

Hamilton, Neil. *Militias in America.* Santa Barbara: ABC-CLIO, Inc., 1996.

Kushner, Harvey W., Ph.D., Ed. *The Future of Terrorism: Violence in the New Millennium.* London: Sage Publications, 1998.

Kushner, Harvey W., Ph.D. *Terrorism in America.* Springfield, IL: Charles C. Thomas Publisher, Ltd., 1998.

Marighella, Carlos. *Urban Guerrilla Minimanual.* Vancouver: Pulp Press, 1974.

Mizell, Louis R. Jr. *Target USA.* New York: John Wiley and Son, Inc., 1998.

Pierce, William. *The Turner Diaries.* Hillsboro, WV: Vanguard Books, 1978.

Snow, Robert L. *The Militia Threat: Terrorist Among Us.* New York: Plenum Trade, 1999.

Reports

Federal Bureau of Investigation. *Project Megiddo: An Analysis.* 1999.

Terrorism in the United States: 1998. Washington DC: Counterterrorism Threat
      Assessment and Warning Unit, National Security Division, Federal Bureau of
      Investigation, (undated, 1998).

Periodicals

Barton, Donna. "Ruby Ridge Survivor Draws Crowd to Gun, Knife Show." *The
News Leader* (Springfield, MO), 31 January 2000.

Cooper, Marc. "Y2K and the Militia Right: Whoopee, We're All Gonna Die…Rich!"
      The Nation 269, no. i6 (23 August 1999):21.

Duffy, James E., and Alan C. Brantley, M.A. "Militias: Initiating Contact." *FBI Law
      Enforcement Bulletin*, (July 1997): 4-6.

Flynn, Kevin. "Two Men Indicted in Explosives Inquiry: One-time Militia Leader,
      Businessman Accused of Selling Devices to Agents." *Denver Rocky Mountain
      News*, 22 July 2000, 6A.

Kaplan, David E. and Mike Tharp. "Terrorism Threats at Home: Two Years After
      Oklahoma City, Violent Sects Abound." *U. S. News and World Report* 123,
      no, 25 (29 December 1997): 22.

Mariani, Mack. "The Michigan Militia: Political Engagement or Political Alienation."
      Terrorism and Political Violence, 10, no. 4 (Winter 1998): 125.

"Militia Terror." *Maclean's* 111, no. 3 (19 January 1998): 62.

Owen, Penny. "FBI Says Dozens of Attacks Foiled." *The Daily Oklahoman*, 16 April
      2000, 9A.

Reardon, Kate. "County Prepares for Possible Terrorism." *Daily Herald*, Everett
      (WA), 27 October 2000.

Ruelas, Richard. "FBI Agent: Arizona Hotbed of Militias." *The Arizona Republic*
      (Phoenix), 24 January 1999, A15.

Walter, Erin. "Militias Want Destruction, Not Reform." *Lewiston Morning Tribune* (ID), 11 December 1999.

On-line Sources

"Attorney Morris Dees Pioneer in Using 'Damage Litigation' to Fight Hate Groups." *CNN*, 8 September 2000. *American On Line.* Under the keyword "Dees." Accessed 25 September 2000.

"Calendar of Conspiracy: A Chronology of Anti-Government Extremist Criminal Activity." *The Militia Watchdog* 2, no. 4 (October-December 1998), URL: <http://www.militia-watchdog.org/cocv2n4.html.> Accessed 15 January 2001.

"Convicted Oklahoma City Bomber Timothy McVeigh, on Federal Death Row for the Deadliest Act of Terrorism in U. S. history, Wants to Stop His Court Appeals and Ask the President for Clemency." *MSNBC*, 13 December 2000. *MSN.COM.*
Under the keyword "McVeigh." Accessed on 24 December 2000.

De Armond, Paul. "Militias and CLUE Activity in Whatcom and Snohomish Counties," 1996. *Militia Chronology*, URL: <http://nwcitizen.com/publicgood/reports/militiachron.html>. Accessed 2 April 2001.

"Extremist Right-wing Ideas Find Another Outlet." *Montana Human Rights Network*, May 2000, URL: <http://www.mhrn.org>. Accessed 16 November 2000.

"Intelligence Report," Fall 2000. *Southern Poverty Law Center.* URL: <http://www.splcenter.org/intelligenceproject/ip-mainbtm.html>. Accessed 19 February 2001.

Kreps, Ken. "Militias-Armed and Deadly," 28 September 2000. *Themestream*, URL: <http://www.themestream.com/gspd>. Accessed on 16 November 2000.

"Militia of Montana Online Information Center," *Militia of Montana*, URL: <http://www.militiaofmontana.com>. Accessed 16 November 2000.

"Mystery Witness Sought in Amtrak Derailment." *CNN*, 14 October 1995. *America On Line.* Under the keywords "Sunset Limited." accessed 10 January 2001.

Stern, Kenneth S. "Militias and the Religious Right." October 1996. *Institute for First Amendment Studies, Inc,.* URL: <http://www.ifas.org/fw/9610/militias.html>. Downloaded 25 September 2000.